PUFFIN BOOKS

THE GINGERBREAD MAN

It's nearly midnight, and all is dark and still in the kitchen. The dresser folk are fast asleep – all except for Herr Von Cuckoo, that is. He is inside his cuckoo clock, getting ready to cuckoo twelve times. The first four 'cuckoos' are loud and clear, but then disaster strikes ... Herr Von Cuckoo starts to lose his voice! Soon Herr Von Cuckoo's friends, Miss Pepper and Mr Salt, are awake and trying desperately to think of a cure for a sore throat – for everyone knows that a cuckoo clock cuckoo that cannot 'cuckoo' is a likely candidate for the Dustbin! Then they find a freshly baked Gingerbread Man who comes to life when he's given currants for eyes and a nose and a red cherry for a mouth. And it's the Gingerbread Man's bright ideas and courageous efforts that save Herr Von Cuckoo from the dreaded Dustbin!

David Wood is Britain's leading children's playwright, with nearly twenty plays to his credit. The plays are produced all over the world and tour in the UK with his own Whirligig Theatre. He is also an actor.

DAVID WOOD

The Gingerbread Man

Illustrated by Sally Anne Lambert

PUFFIN BOOKS

Puffin Books, Penguin Books Ltd, 27 Wrights Lane, London W8 5TZ (Publishing and Editorial)
and Harmondsworth, Middlesex, England (Distribution and Warehouse)
Viking Penguin Inc., 40 West 23rd Street, New York, New York 10010, USA
Penguin Books Australia Ltd, Ringwood, Victoria, Australia
Penguin Books Canada Ltd, 2801 John Street, Markham, Ontario, Canada L3R 1B4
Penguin Books (NZ) Ltd, 182–190 Wairau Road, Auckland 10, New Zealand

Text first published by Pavilion Books Limited 1985
This edition published in Puffin Books 1987

Text copyright © David Wood, 1985
Illustrations copyright © Sally Anne Lambert, 1987
This story is based on David Wood's musical play *The Gingerbread Man*,
which is published by Samuel French Limited
All rights reserved

Made and printed in Great Britain by
Richard Clay Ltd, Bungay, Suffolk
Filmset in Baskerville

for Katherine and Rebecca

Chapter 1

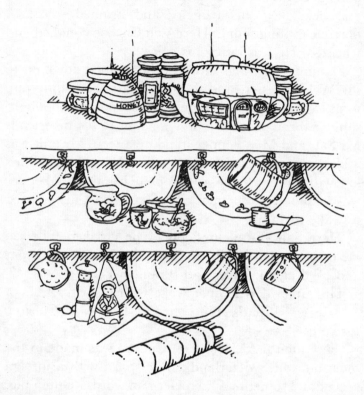

In the kitchen, all was dark and still. It was nearly midnight. But Herr Von Cuckoo was wide awake. Inside his cuckoo clock he was getting ready to cuckoo the time. At exactly the right moment he popped out of his front door and took a deep breath.

'Cuckoo! Cuckoo! Cuckoo! Cuckoo!' He called loud and clear.

'Cuckoo! Cuckoo! Cuckoo! Cuckoo!' Now it was

rather an effort. His voice sounded husky. Herr Von Cuckoo frowned.

'Cuckoo! Cuck . . . oo!' His voice cracked. 'Cuck . . . oo!' He could hardly sing the notes now. 'C . . . c . . . c . . . cuck . . .' – he struggled and strained – 'oo!' A horrible grating sound. Herr Von Cuckoo coughed and wheezed. He was losing his voice.

Flapping his wings in fright, he jumped down on to the Welsh dresser, and, hopping past the rolling-pin, went to look for help. There was just enough moonlight shining through the window for him to see his friends Mr Salt and Miss Pepper standing asleep. Mr Salt was a blue and white striped salt-cellar. He wore a sailor's hat with holes for the salt to pour from. Miss Pepper was a shapely red pepper mill. Herr Von Cuckoo tried to wake them up.

'Herr Salt, Fräulein Pepper,' he croaked. Silence. He couldn't call loudly enough. He cleared his throat and tried again. 'Herr Salt, Fräulein Pepper!'

This time Miss Pepper woke with a start. 'A . . . a . . . atishoo! What's going on? Oh, Herr Von Cuckoo, it's you.'

'Ja. Guten tag.' Herr Von Cuckoo was made in the mountains of Switzerland, so he spoke with a foreign accent and sometimes used German words. 'Guten tag, good day.'

Before Miss Pepper could reply, she felt something heavy leaning against her. A large envelope.

'Oh no,' she cried, 'the Big Ones have done it again! I refuse to be used as a letter rack!'

The Big Ones were the human beings who owned the kitchen. They had put the letter in between Mr Salt and Miss Pepper before going upstairs to bed.

'Mr Salt! Mr Salt!' shouted Miss Pepper, as she pushed the envelope towards him. He woke with a start, and felt the envelope falling.

'Shiver me timbers! Storm to starboard! Ready about! Man the lifeboats! We're running aground! SOS!' He struggled with the envelope.

'It's all right, Mr Salt,' said Miss Pepper. 'We're not running aground. You were having one of your nautical nightmares.'

'Sorry, Miss Pepper. I dreamed the windblown sails were enveloping us.'

'No, Mr Salt, we are being enveloped by an envelope. Kindly remove it.'

'Ah. Aye, aye, ma'am.'

Mr Salt struggled to lift it to one side and Herr Von Cuckoo helped.

'Thank you, shipmate,' said Mr Salt. 'Couldn't have heave-hoed it on my own. Good morrow to you!'

'Guten tag,' whispered Herr Von Cuckoo.

'What can we do for you, shipmate?'

'I have my voice lost,' croaked Herr Von Cuckoo.

Mr Salt and Miss Pepper discussed the problem. Mr Salt suggested that Herr Von Cuckoo should have a rest and stop 'cuckoo-ing' for a few days.

'Impossible,' replied Herr Von Cuckoo. 'Is my job.'

Miss Pepper agreed and rather unkindly pointed out that a cuckoo clock cuckoo that cannot 'cuckoo' is nothing short of useless. 'If you ask me, Mr Salt,' she said firmly, 'Cuckoo could be a likely candidate for the Dustbin.'

There was a horrible silence. Then Herr Von Cuckoo started flapping his wings in terror. 'Nein, nein, no, no, please!' he squawked. 'Not the Dustbin!'

Mr Salt jumped to his rescue. 'Calm down, Cuckoo, *calm*. What a cruel thing to say, Miss Pepper.'

'I'm only being realistic,' insisted Miss Pepper. 'What do the Big Ones do when they've finished with something or if something doesn't work? Throw it in the Dustbin.' Herr Von Cuckoo trembled. 'Bang. The end. Never seen again.'

They all knew this was true. Miss Pepper wasn't the sort to hide the truth however much it might hurt. If Herr Von Cuckoo couldn't get his voice back soon, the Big Ones wouldn't be able to hear him announce the time – and that could easily lead him to the dreaded Dustbin.

Mr Salt had an idea. 'He must go on leave,' he exclaimed. 'To the seaside.' He turned to Herr Von Cuckoo in excitement. 'Get some salty sea air in your lungs and your voice will come back loud as a fog-horn.'

Miss Pepper looked at him scornfully. 'How do *you* know?' she cried. 'You've never seen the sea. The near-est the sea *you've* ever been was that willow-pattern sauce-boat on the top shelf of the dresser. And what happened to that? One day the Big Ones found it was cracked and – bang –'

'– the Dustbin.' Gloomily Mr Salt finished the sen-tence for her.

Then he became excited again. 'All the more reason for Cuckoo to see the real sea,' he cried. 'I've had salt in me all my life and I've never lost my voice. Go on, shipmate. Weigh anchor and fly away.'

Herr Von Cuckoo sadly shook his head. 'You forget,' he croaked. 'I cannot fly. My wings are wooden.' He began to weep with despair.

Mr Salt turned to Miss Pepper. 'You shouldn't have mentioned the Dustbin,' he whispered.

Miss Pepper could see how upset Herr Von Cuckoo was. She realized she had spoken too honestly and tried to apologize. 'Herr Von Cuckoo, I was very unkind. But standing on the work top all day I get so bored and bad-tempered. When night-time comes I take it out on my friends. I'm sorry. Forgive me?'

After a pause, Herr Von Cuckoo kissed Miss Pepper gently on both cheeks to show he accepted her apology. Then he turned and thoughtfully hopped back past the rolling-pin towards his cuckoo clock.

Mr Salt and Miss Pepper settled down to sleep again. But not for long.

'Herr Salt! Fräulein Pepper!' called Cuckoo urgently. 'Schnell, schnell!'

'Smell, what smell?' said Mr Salt. 'What's he croaking about?'

'Schnell,' said Miss Pepper. 'That's Cuckoo's word for quick.'

They rushed over to Herr Von Cuckoo who was looking behind the rolling-pin, flapping his wings with excitement. He had found something.

'Was ist das? What is that?' he asked.

They saw a small brown man lying on the dresser. Mr Salt gave it a gentle prod. 'It's warm,' he said.

'Let's heave-ho it on to the rolling-pin and have a proper look.'

'It's a Gingerbread Man!' cried Miss Pepper. 'The Big Ones must have baked him.'

The Gingerbread Man sat motionless on the rolling-pin. He showed no sign of life. There was something strange about him. He had no face.

'Let's finish him,' said Miss Pepper.

'Yes,' said Herr Von Cuckoo. 'Let's give him eyes and mouth and nose.'

So they searched the dresser for things they could use. They found currants for his eyes and nose, and a

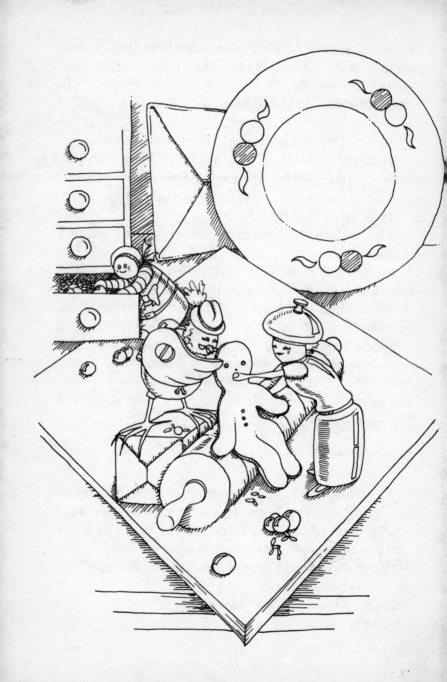

large red cherry for his mouth. Carefully they pushed them into his biscuity head. They made an excellent cheeky face.

But the Gingerbread Man still showed no sign of life.

'Is he all right?' whispered Herr Von Cuckoo.

'No, he's all wrong,' said Mr Salt. 'Why won't he wake up? He's got all his tackle.'

'I know!' said Miss Pepper. 'Make him sneeze.'

'How?' asked Mr Salt.

'Me,' replied Miss Pepper. 'Kindly twist my grinder a touch.'

Mr Salt did so, making a few little peppercorns drop out of Miss Pepper. They picked them up and rubbed them under the Gingerbread Man's new nose. They waited.

Suddenly the Gingerbread Man moved. 'A . . . a . . . atishoo!' The pepper made him sneeze. The sneeze made him wake up, and waking up made him curious. He slowly stood up and started moving his arms and legs with delight. Then he jumped in the air.

The others introduced themselves. The Gingerbread Man shook them all by the hand, and with a great effort, started to talk.

'H-ha-hall-o. Ha-llo. Hallo, Salt. Hallo, Pepper. Hallo, Herr Von Cuckoo!' As his voice became clearer it became louder too. And leaping up and down with excitement he nearly knocked everyone over. 'Hallo! Hallo! Hallo! Hallo!'

'Maybe we made his mouth a little large,' whispered Miss Pepper.

'No, no,' said Mr Salt. 'Only the excitement of his first voyage.'

The Gingerbread Man came bounding back. 'I say, where am I?' he yelled.

'In the kitchen,' said Mr Salt.

'On the dresser,' said Miss Pepper.

'You are a Gingerbread Man. Baked freshly,' said Herr Von Cuckoo.

'Baked freshly?' shouted the Gingerbread Man.

'By the Big Ones,' said Mr Salt.

'The Big Ones?' yelled the Gingerbread Man.

'Talking of whom, I wonder, shipmate,' said Mr Salt nervously, 'could you turn down the volume a little? If they should wake up . . .'

'Certainly, Salty!' cried the Gingerbread Man, just as loudly. 'Ha, ha! Say no more!' He slapped Mr Salt on the back and bounced off to explore his new home. He tried to move a big plate leaning against the back of the dresser.

'Hey, mind that plate!' called Mr Salt.

Miss Pepper found it funny. But not for long. Suddenly the Gingerbread Man spotted a sort of box with knobs on.

'I say, Salty, what's this?'

'That, shipmate? Nothing special. It's a transistor radio. I wouldn't touch it if I . . .' But it was too late. The Gingerbread Man flicked a knob and music started blaring out.

The Gingerbread Man listened for a moment, then started leaping up and down in time with the music. The others stared at him. They were horrified. The music was so noisy that it couldn't be long before . . .

and sure enough they suddenly heard other noises. Muffled thudding sounds. The Big Ones had woken up and were coming downstairs.

Mr Salt dashed to the transistor radio, turned it off, and ran back to join Miss Pepper. Herr Von Cuckoo scurried back to his clock. He slammed his front door in the nick of time. For now the kitchen door opened and a blinding light hit the dresser. Mrs Big One had turned the kitchen light on. Mr Big One followed her into the kitchen.

The Gingerbread Man was dazzled by the light. He had no idea what was going on and stood frozen to the spot.

'Hey, Gingerbread Man!' whispered Mr Salt out of the corner of his mouth. 'Down! Get down!'

The Gingerbread Man understood. He lay down behind the rolling-pin, where the Big Ones had left him.

'THERE YOU ARE, DEAR, NOTHING,' boomed Mrs Big One crossly.

'EXTRAORDINARY, DARLING,' echoed Mr Big One. 'I COULD HAVE SWORN I HEARD THE RADIO BLARING OUT MUSIC.'

'WELL, YOU WERE WRONG, WEREN'T

YOU?' said Mrs Big One. 'IT MUST HAVE COME FROM NEXT DOOR.'

'I SUPPOSE SO,' said Mr Big One.

'COME ON,' said Mrs Big One impatiently, 'LET'S GO BACK TO BED. I'M GETTING COLD.'

As they turned to leave the kitchen, the hands on the cuckoo clock pointed to exactly one o'clock. Herr Von Cuckoo popped out and cleared his throat. 'Cu-ck – ck-oooo,' he called in a cracked, husky voice.

'WHAT A WEEDY LITTLE NOISE,' boomed Mrs Big One.

'NEEDS A BIT OF OIL, MAYBE,' suggested Mr Big One.

'PAST IT MORE LIKE,' said Mrs Big One. 'HAVE TO GET RID OF IT, IF IT CAN'T DO BETTER THAN THAT.'

The kitchen light snapped out and the door slammed. The Big Ones' feet could be heard clomping back upstairs. Then silence.

Herr Von Cuckoo trembled. 'Have to get rid of it, she said,' he kept repeating to himself. But the others were too busy to notice. The Gingerbread Man stood up. 'What happened?' he asked.

Mr Salt was very angry. 'Gingerbread Man,' he said, 'you woke up the Big Ones, that's what happened. Now listen. You're very young, the youngest member of the crew. You were only baked today. But this ship will sink if you . . .'

'Please, Mr Salt, let me,' interrupted Miss Pepper. 'Gingerbread Man, you're very welcome here, but we dresser folk, for our own good, should never cross with the Big Ones.'

'I'm sorry,' said the Gingerbread Man.

'They can be very cruel,' said Miss Pepper.

Herr Von Cuckoo joined them. He was sobbing.

'Cheer up, Cuckoo,' said Mr Salt.

'Did you not hear?' cried Herr Von Cuckoo. 'They will throw me in the Dustbin.'

'What's the Dustbin?' asked the Gingerbread Man.

Miss Pepper explained. 'Anything they don't want, the Big Ones throw in the Dustbin and it's never seen again.'

Herr Von Cuckoo sobbed even more.

'Sorry, Cuckoo,' said Miss Pepper, 'but he must be told.'

'Why should they want to throw Cuckoo away?' asked the Gingerbread Man.

'Because,' sobbed Herr Von Cuckoo, 'I have a toad in the throat.'

'I think you mean frog, shipmate,' said Mr Salt.

'Frog, toad, what is the difference?' wailed Herr Von Cuckoo.

'Well, a toad is larger, with fatter cheeks . . .' At this Herr Von Cuckoo broke down completely.

'I'm sorry, shipmate,' said Mr Salt. 'Most unfeeling.'

'The point is,' said Miss Pepper, 'he can't sing his cuckoos. He's a cuckoo-less cuckoo clock cuckoo.'

The situation seemed hopeless.

Suddenly the Gingerbread Man had an idea.

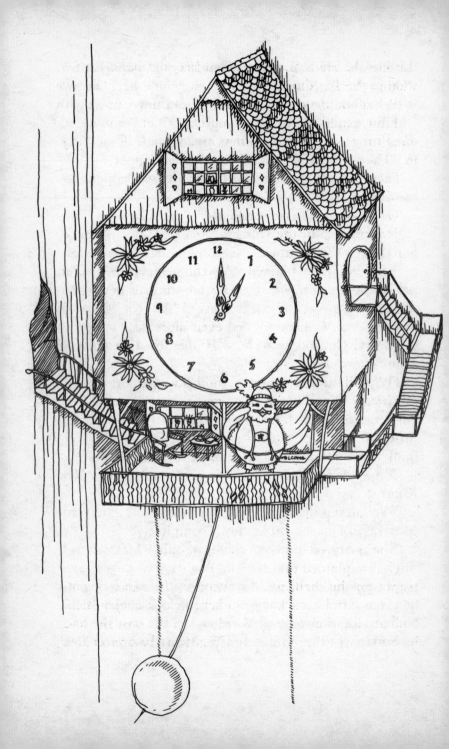

'Listen,' he said. 'Let me help. Let me make up for waking the Big Ones.'

'What could *you* do?' croaked Herr Von Cuckoo.

'Find something to make you better. There must be something on the dresser that could help. Something to soothe your sore throat.'

They all thought hard. Then Miss Pepper remembered.

'Of course,' she cried. 'Honey!'

'Honey!' said the Gingerbread Man. 'What's honey?'

'You eat it. It's soft and sweet and smooth. The perfect thing.'

'Where can I find some?' asked the Gingerbread Man.

Mr Salt looked uncertain. 'It means a voyage of exploration to the High Shelf.'

They all looked up to the shelf above. There sat the honey pot. It was a long way to climb but the Gingerbread Man didn't seem to mind.

Before he set off on his adventure, the others gave him a solemn warning. 'Beware of the Old Bag.'

'The Old Bag? What's that?' asked the Gingerbread Man.

'The most horrible, ruthless ... tea bag,' replied Miss Pepper.

'The terror of the High Shelf,' said Mr Salt.

They explained that the Old Bag lived in the cottage teapot on the shelf, not far away from the honey pot. She was an old tea bag who kept herself to her shelf. Nobody was welcome up there and in the past she had been known to creep out and frighten any dresser folk who had dared visit her. The Gingerbread Man had better watch out. The Old Bag didn't like trespassers.

'Hate oozes out of her perforations,' said Mr Salt. 'Doesn't it, Cuckoo?'

Herr Von Cuckoo opened his mouth to reply. Nothing came out. He tried again. Not a sound. He had no voice left at all. Mr Salt gently led him back to his cuckoo clock. 'Come on, shipmate,' he said. 'I'll take you home.'

Miss Pepper turned to the Gingerbread Man. 'The honey! Please,' she said. 'We'll have to hurry. It's an emergency now.'

The Gingerbread Man eagerly bounced up and down saying,

'Certainly, certainly, quick as I can,
You can rely on the Gingerbread Man!'

Chapter 2

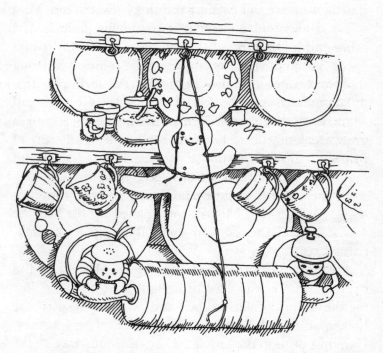

The Gingerbread Man started to try and climb. But the shelf was too high. He jumped as high as he could, but he still couldn't reach. He tried piling up sugar lumps from the sugar bowl and using them as steps, but they wobbled and he fell off. After his third unsuccessful attempt, Mr Salt returned. 'You'll never get up there like that,' he said.

'Think of a better way,' said Miss Pepper.

Mr Salt thought. What would a real old salt of the sea do in this situation? 'Got it!' he cried. 'A capstan!'

'What's a capstan?' asked the Gingerbread Man. Mr Salt showed him. He found some string that had come tied round a parcel for the Big Ones and, throwing it up, managed to loop it over a cup-hook on the edge of the shelf above. Then he gave the Gingerbread Man one end and told him to tie it round his middle. The other end he tied round the rolling-pin. All was ready.

Mr Salt and Miss Pepper rolled the rolling-pin along the work top, and this tightened the string, which pulled over the cup-hook and hoisted the Gingerbread Man slowly but surely up towards the shelf. It took a great deal of effort, but eventually the Gingerbread Man, dangling from the string, reached the shelf and managed to scramble on to it. He removed the loop from around his middle and hung it from the cup-hook. Mr Salt and Miss Pepper looked up to check he was safe, and then sat on the rolling-pin for a well-earned rest.

Treading on tiptoe, the Gingerbread Man started to explore. There was very little light, but he could just see the shapes of various jars and pots. He spotted the honey, and not far from it, the Old Bag's teapot. Careful not to make any noise, he made his way to the honey pot, and started to lift off the lid. He could smell the honey inside. 'This will make Cuckoo's voice come back in no time,' he thought. He leaned over the side of the pot and prepared to scoop out a good handful. He didn't hear the lid of the cottage teapot creak menacingly open and he didn't see the Old Bag peeping out. But the Old Bag saw him. She saw a stranger stealing her honey. So, silently, like a ghost, she crept out of the teapot towards the Gingerbread Man.

She pounced! He jumped! She grabbed him! He dropped the honey back in the pot.

'Who are you?' asked the Old Bag sharply.

'The G-G-G-Gingerbread Man,' replied the Gingerbread Man nervously.

'Never heard of you,' snapped the Old Bag.

'I was only b-b-baked today,' said the Gingerbread Man. 'By the Big Ones.'

'You're trespassing,' said the Old Bag. 'This is *my* shelf.'

'But this is an emergency,' cried the Gingerbread Man. 'Herr Von Cuckoo . . .'

'What about him?' interrupted the Old Bag.

'He's lost his voice,' said the Gingerbread Man.

The Old Bag smiled. 'You mean he can't cuckoo?'

'Yes! I mean no!' said the Gingerbread Man.

The Old Bag cackled an evil cackle.

'So I thought . . .' went on the Gingerbread Man.

'What did you think?' snapped the Old Bag.

'I thought I'd get him some honey,' said the Gingerbread Man. 'It might help him.'

The Old Bag smiled again. A cruel smile.

'You thought wrong,' she sneered.

'You mean honey won't help him?' asked the Gingerbread Man.

'I mean you're not getting him any!' squealed the Old Bag. 'I'm glad, delighted he's lost his voice. I've always hated that stupid noise every hour of the day and night. "Cuckoo, cuckoo, cuckoo." Now perhaps I can get a bit of peace and quiet.'

'But the Big Ones may throw him in the Dustbin,' pleaded the Gingerbread Man.

'Good riddance,' spat the Old Bag. 'And good riddance to you, too. Clear off! I never want to see you again.'

'Why not?' asked the Gingerbread Man.

'Because you don't like me.'

'How do you know?'

'Nobody likes me,' muttered the Old Bag. 'I'm all alone. All the other tea bags in my packet were used up ages ago. The Big Ones missed me and I hid in the teapot. No one ever visits me.'

'Well, it's not easy getting here,' said the Gingerbread Man.

'It's not easy living here,' complained the Old Bag.

The Gingerbread Man thought for a moment. 'Are you lonely?' he asked.

'I never said that,' snapped the Old Bag. But the Gingerbread Man could tell she was. Very lonely. 'I'll be your friend,' he said.

'Huh,' said the Old Bag. 'Bribery. Let's be friends. Then I give you the honey. Whoosh, down. Never see you again.'

'I don't think you want a friend,' said the Gingerbread Man, turning to go.

'I never said that,' snapped the Old Bag. 'I'm quite enjoying a bit of company.'

She smiled at the Gingerbread Man. 'I'll tell your fortune for you, if you like.'

'Will you? How?'

'Tea leaves have always had special magic fortune-telling powers. They send messages through my perforations. Show me your hand.'

'Well . . .' The Gingerbread Man hesitated.

'Come along,' said the Old Bag, 'don't be shy.'

The Gingerbread Man nervously held out his hand. The Old Bag studied it carefully.

'What can you see?' whispered the Gingerbread Man.

'A message,' replied the Old Bag mysteriously.

'For me?'

'Yes. Listen and learn.' She concentrated hard, and slowly chanted the message.

'When trouble comes, if you can cope
Three lives will shortly find new hope.'

The Gingerbread Man was puzzled. 'What does it mean?' he asked.

'You'll find out,' said the Old Bag. 'Soon.'

'Thank you, Old Bag.'

'Don't thank me. Thank the power of the tea leaves.'

The Old Bag was beginning to enjoy herself with her new visitor. She invited him to look around her shelf. She showed him her herb garden. In glass storage jars were all the herbs you could think of. Sage, rosemary, thyme, marjoram, dill, chives, bay, bilberry and many more.

'What are they for?' asked the Gingerbread Man.

'They contain remarkable medicinal powers,' explained the Old Bag. 'I have studied them hard and long. They can cure diseases, make sick folk better.'

'Nobody told me you could do that,' said the Gingerbread Man.

'Nobody else knows,' said the Old Bag.

'But think of the good you could do for the dresser folk,' said the Gingerbread Man, 'the help you could be.'

'Nobody's ever asked for my help,' muttered the Old Bag.

'I'm asking you now,' cried the Gingerbread Man. 'To help Cuckoo.'

'That noisy bird?' shrieked the Old Bag, getting angry again.

'Just a small lump of honey . . .'

'No, no, no! I must be getting soft. I was beginning to like you. But you weren't being friendly at all.'

'I was!' said the Gingerbread Man.

'All you want is your rotten honey,' screeched the Old Bag. 'And if I give you some I'll never see you again.'

'You will. I'll come back,' said the Gingerbread Man.

'Clear off!' yelled the Old Bag. 'Get off my shelf!' And she stomped back to her cottage teapot and slammed the door.

The Gingerbread Man sadly turned to leave. He looked at the honey pot. He thought of poor Herr Von Cuckoo's toad in the throat. He looked at the Old Bag's teapot. The door was firmly shut. Should he steal the honey? It really seemed the right thing to do. But he'd feel guilty about it. If only the Old Bag hadn't been so mean. 'She'd never notice,' he thought. 'Not if I only took *one* handful. And Herr Von Cuckoo needs it so much.'

He made up his mind and tiptoed towards the honey pot. Reaching down inside, he scooped up the honey. He looked over at the teapot. The door was still closed. Carefully he carried the honey to the edge of the shelf. He looked over the edge to the work top below. Mr Salt and Miss Pepper were half asleep on the rolling-pin. 'Salty!' he whispered. 'Miss Pepper! Pssst!' He whispered as loud as he dared. 'Salty! Pssssst!'

'Atishoo!' Miss Pepper woke with a sneeze. The sneeze woke Mr Salt. They both looked up, saw the Gingerbread Man and understood what was happening. They ran to the back of the dresser and brought out one of the large patterned plates leaning there. They held it out below the shelf, and the Gingerbread Man prepared to throw down the honey. He didn't see the Old Bag peeping from under the teapot lid.

'You double-crossing little thief!' she shouted. 'Just let me get my hands on you!'

In a fury she stomped towards the Gingerbread Man, who quickly threw the honey down to the work top, found the loop of string hanging round the cup-hook, and slipped it over his head and arms. Down below, Mr Salt and Miss Pepper caught the honey on the plate, stowed it safely to one side, and manned the rolling-pin capstan once more.

The Old Bag reached the Gingerbread Man and made a grab for him. But, in the nick of time, he jumped off the shelf and hung in mid-air dangling from the string. By rolling back the rolling-pin, Mr Salt and Miss Pepper lowered him jerkily to safety.

'You evil little trickster!' screeched the Old Bag. 'Stealing deserves punishment and punished you will be!'

She flung herself down on to the shelf, in a last vain attempt to grasp him. The Gingerbread Man dropped safely to the work top. Mr Salt and Miss Pepper helped him take off the loop of string.

'You won't get away with it, you know,' sneered the Old Bag up above. 'Gingerbread Man. Can you hear me? You'll soon suffer. You won't be around much longer.'

The Gingerbread Man listened.

'The Big Ones bake Gingerbread Men,' continued

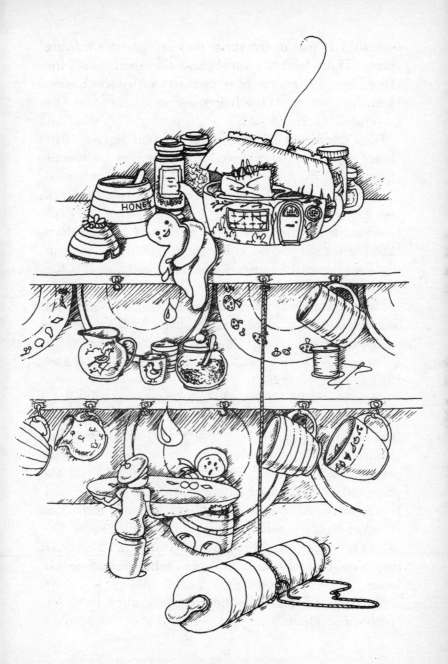

the Old Bag, 'to eat them. While they're fresh and tasty. Eat them! Goodbye, Gingerbread Man. Goodbye for ever!' She cackled with delight and scampered back to her teapot.

The Gingerbread Man was stunned. Mr Salt and Miss Pepper led him gently to the rolling-pin. 'Is it true?' he asked. 'Am I going to be eaten by the Big Ones?'

Mr Salt hesitated. 'Well, shipmate,' he said, 'we can't say for certain . . .'

'But,' interrupted Miss Pepper, 'well, normally, if the Big Ones bake anything, they . . .'

'I see,' said the Gingerbread Man quietly.

'Sorry, shipmate,' said Mr Salt.

'We didn't say anything because . . . well, you seemed so happy,' said Miss Pepper. 'And you cheered all of us up.'

'*And* you were brave enough to answer Cuckoo's SOS,' added Mr Salt.

'Cuckoo!' The Gingerbread Man jumped up. 'I must tell him we've got his honey.' He set off towards the cuckoo clock. He was determined not to be upset by the Old Bag's words. 'Don't worry about me!' he smiled back at the others. 'I'm not beaten . . . till I'm eaten! And I won't be eaten . . . till I'm beaten!'

He knocked on the cuckoo clock door. Herr Von Cuckoo hobbled out, looking pale and ill.

'Don't speak!' said the Gingerbread Man. 'Save your voice. Just to let you know I fetched some honey. For your throat.' He pointed over to the plate.

Herr Von Cuckoo smiled gratefully, then turned to go back inside.

'Aren't you going to eat it?' asked the Gingerbread Man.

Herr Von Cuckoo shook his head. He pointed to the clock which said ten minutes to two. In ten minutes' time he must cuckoo the hour.

'Can't you give it a miss this once?' said the Gingerbread Man. 'You're not well.'

Herr Von Cuckoo shook his head again. His duty came first.

'All right,' said the Gingerbread Man. 'But you'll try the honey afterwards?'

Herr Von Cuckoo nodded and turned back towards his clock.

'Fine,' said the Gingerbread Man.

> 'Your throat is sore, you're feeling sick –
> A dose of honey will do the trick!'

Chapter 3

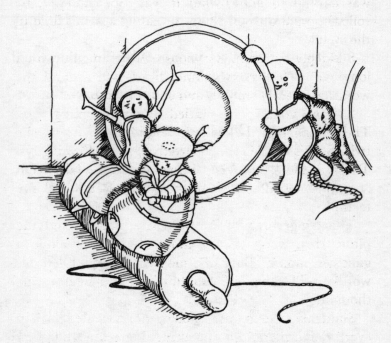

Herr Von Cuckoo went back inside his clock. The Gingerbread Man was tired after his exciting voyage to the High Shelf, so he joined Mr Salt and Miss Pepper on the rolling-pin, yawned, and started nodding off to sleep.

Suddenly he woke with a start. What was that strange noise? A sort of scratching, scuffling noise. It stopped. Then it started again. It appeared to come from behind the dresser. Mr Salt and Miss Pepper were fast asleep, so the Gingerbread Man decided to investigate on his own. He tracked down the noise to behind one of the large patterned plates leaning against the back of the dresser. The scratching and scuffling seemed to get louder. The Gingerbread Man was curious to know what it was. So, carefully, he rolled the plate to one side, revealing a small hole in the wood.

Suddenly out popped a mouse. A grey mouse with a long tail. Whiskers twitching, he darted around the work top eagerly sniffing and snuffling.

'O guys you K,' he snarled in a threatening way. Then, realizing that didn't sound quite right, he twitched his whiskers and started again. 'O K you guys. This is a raid. One move and you'll feel my false teeth . . . no, I mean, one false move and you'll feel my teeth!'

The Gingerbread Man watched from behind the plate. He'd never seen a mouse before, let alone a gangster mouse. But any mouse who muddled his words up like this one couldn't be too dangerous, he thought.

Suddenly, the mouse sniffed more excitedly than ever. 'Somewhere,' he squeaked, 'I snack a sniff . . . I mean, sniff a snack. A lip-smackin', paw-lickin', whisker-itchin', nose-twitchin' supersnack. And I'm gonna track it down. For days my belly's been empty and I've had a bellyful!'

He sniffed along the work top in search of food. The Gingerbread Man thought he had better introduce himself. He ran up to the mouse. 'Hallo!' he said with a smile. The mouse jumped back in fright, then collected himself and tried to look tough.

'You're standing in my way, stranger,' he drawled.

'I'm the Gingerbread Man,' said the Gingerbread Man, holding out a hand of friendship. The mouse hesitated, then nervously held out a paw. Hand shook paw.

'Hi, Ginger,' said the mouse. 'I'm Sleek the Mouse. And I'm telling you this dresser ain't big enough for both of us.'

'I don't know what you mean,' said the Gingerbread Man.

Sleek suddenly sniffed his paw. He could smell something good to eat. What was it? Then it clicked. This delicious smell had come from the Gingerbread Man's handshake. 'Hey,' squealed Sleek, wide-eyed with anticipation. 'It's you! You're my little snackeroo!'

'What?' said the Gingerbread Man, sensing danger.

Sleek stepped closer. 'You smell good enough to eat, Ginger.'

'I am,' said the Gingerbread Man, backing away. 'But not by you!' He scampered off as fast as his legs would go. Sleek chased after him. Round and round the transistor radio. Past the plates. Over the work top. Suddenly the Gingerbread Man stopped, terrified. He was right on the edge of the work top. One more step and he would fall off on to the kitchen floor below. Sleek saw his chance. He pounced. With a huge effort, the Gingerbread Man jumped to one side. Sleek landed half-way over the edge. It was his turn to be terrified.

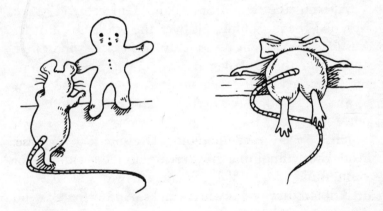

Desperately clinging on he managed to scramble back up. Angry and shaken he took up the chase again. The Gingerbread Man doubled back round the transistor radio then sped over towards the rolling-pin. 'Help, help!' he cried.

Mr Salt and Miss Pepper woke up and saw what was happening. They rushed to help. Miss Pepper managed to position herself between Sleek and the Gingerbread Man. She twisted her grinder, picked up the pepper that dropped out, and threw it towards Sleek, who sniffed it, paused, then sneezed violently. 'Atishoo!'

Meanwhile Mr Salt decided the Gingerbread Man would be safer on the High Shelf. He threw the loop of string over the Gingerbread Man's head, and, heaving and straining, rolled the rolling-pin which hoisted the Gingerbread Man to the shelf above.

Sleek recovered from his sneezing and started chasing Mr Salt and Miss Pepper.

Safe on the High Shelf, the Gingerbread Man watched them scuffling all over the work top. But he wasn't safe for long. Suddenly the teapot door flew open, and the Old Bag dashed out. 'Honey-stealer!' she screamed. 'I'll teach you!' And she chased him in and out among the herb jars and round the honey pot.

There was pandemonium. Dresser folk chasing everywhere. Shouting and screaming.

But suddenly, as if by magic, all was still. All the dresser folk stopped in their tracks. And listened.

Footsteps. Coming down the stairs. The Big Ones!

The Old Bag ran back inside her teapot. Mr Salt and Miss Pepper dashed back to their positions. The Gingerbread Man lay flat out on the High Shelf. He hoped the Big Ones wouldn't notice he had moved from where they had left him. Only Sleek didn't know

what was going on. He had never seen or heard the Big Ones before. So he crouched uncertainly on the work top.

The kitchen door opened and the light went on. A sudden, blinding light. Sleek, dazzled by its brightness, stood transfixed.

Voices resounded from above.

'THERE WAS NO NEED FOR YOU TO COME DOWN, DEAR,' boomed Mrs Big One.

'BUT YOU SAID YOU HEARD NOISES, DARLING,' echoed Mr Big One.

'I DID, DEAR,' said Mrs Big One. 'FUNNY SCUFFLING NOI ... AAAAAAAAAH! LOOK!'

'HEAVENS!' exclaimed Mr Big One. 'A MOUSE!'

'AAAAAAAAAAAAAAAH!' screamed Mrs Big One. She didn't like mice.

Sleek just cowered on the work top, nose twitching, whiskers quivering.

'SHOO! SHOO! YOU VERMINOUS LITTLE RODENT!' shouted Mr Big One. 'SHOO! SHOO!'

Sleek came to his senses. He scurried away behind a plate.

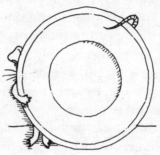

'HE'S GONE, DARLING,' said Mr Big One.
'HE HASN'T!' wailed Mrs Big One. 'HE'S HIDING! UGHHHHHH!'

Mr Big One decided to put down some poison. That would soon get rid of the mouse. He took a tin from a cupboard and sprinkled down the poison on to the work top.

'THIS'LL TEACH YOU, YOU WRETCHED RODENT. ONE GULP AND YOU'RE A GONER!'

Mr and Mrs Big One opened the kitchen door to go. At that moment Herr Von Cuckoo slowly and painfully limped from his clock. It was two o'clock. He croaked twice. Two grating noises, nothing like his usual clear cuckoos.

'HUH!' boomed Mr Big One. 'THAT CUCK-OO'S NO BETTER.'

'I'LL DEAL WITH IT IN THE MORNING, DEAR,' said Mrs Big One.

The bright light snapped off and the dresser folk listened as Mr and Mrs Big One clumped their way upstairs to bed. Sleek swiftly made his escape through his mouse hole. Once again, only the soft moonlight from the window lit up the dresser.

Herr Von Cuckoo looked towards the kitchen door, then at the plate of honey on the work top. 'I'll show the Big Ones,' he thought. 'In the morning, thanks to the Gingerbread Man's honey, I will quite better be!'

He hopped down towards the plate. He didn't notice the poison lying on the work top. He didn't notice that some of it had fallen on the honey. Happily he pecked at it.

'Cuckoo!' From the shelf above, the Gingerbread Man shouted a warning. 'Cuckoo! No!'

'My friend,' croaked Herr Von Cuckoo gratefully. 'How can I thank you? I better already feel.' He pecked at the honey once more.

'No!' shouted the Gingerbread Man.

Mr Salt and Miss Pepper, seeing what was happening, ran over and heaved the plate to one side. Then they used the rolling-pin capstan to quickly lower the Gingerbread Man to the work top.

'Did Cuckoo eat any?' asked Mr Salt.

'One mouthful,' said the Gingerbread Man.

'What is the matter?' asked Herr Von Cuckoo. 'First you honey fetch me, then away it take.'

'It's poisoned, Cuckoo,' said Miss Pepper. 'Poisoned by the Big Ones.'

'No!' Cuckoo smiled. 'You make the bit of a joke with me, yes? I tell you I much better already feel. Listen. Cuckoo! Cuckoo!'

Sure enough his voice sounded much better. But after a couple more cuckoos he clutched his stomach and swayed uncontrollably. Mr Salt caught him as he collapsed in a faint.

45

'Quick, lie him down,' said Miss Pepper.

'Aye, aye, ma'am,' said Mr Salt.

Miss Pepper found a tea cloth and spread it over Herr Von Cuckoo to keep him warm.

'What are we going to do?' asked the Gingerbread Man.

'Nothing much we *can* do,' replied Miss Pepper. 'Just wait and hope he didn't eat too much poison.'

Mr Salt put his ear to Herr Von Cuckoo's chest. 'He's still breathing,' he told the others. 'Just. If only we had a ship's doctor.'

The Gingerbread Man thought for a moment. Then he jumped up with excitement. 'But we have!' he cried.

'What?' said Mr Salt.

'Well, not a doctor exactly,' said the Gingerbread Man, 'but she could help!'

'Who?' said Miss Pepper.

'The Old Bag,' said the Gingerbread Man. 'With her herbs. She told me "They can cure diseases, make sick folk better."'

'She won't come to the rescue,' said Mr Salt gloomily. 'Never has before. Remember that jelly mould, Miss Pepper?'

'Yes,' said Miss Pepper. 'Top shelf she was. In the shape of a rabbit.'

'She was made of metal,' continued Mr Salt. 'One day she started getting rusty. Next day. Bang. The Dustbin. The Old Bag never lifted a leaf to help.'

'But did anyone ask her to help?' said the Gingerbread Man.

'Huh,' replied Miss Pepper, 'no one dared to go near her. Waste of time anyway.'

'Well,' said the Gingerbread Man, 'if you didn't ask her, you could hardly expect her to help.' He looked up towards the teapot. 'Hey! Old Bag!' he called. 'Can you hear me? Old Bag!'

There was no reply.

'It's no use, shipmate.'

Herr Von Cuckoo groaned with pain. Mr Salt and Miss Pepper looked at him. The situation was serious. He felt so ill. And they felt so helpless.

The Gingerbread Man made up his mind. He started putting on the loop of string. 'Come on,' he said, 'hoist me up again. The Old Bag is Cuckoo's only chance.'

'But . . .' started Mr Salt.

'He's right, Mr Salt,' interrupted Miss Pepper. 'Let him try.'

Mr Salt thought for a second.

'Quick!' urged the Gingerbread Man.

'Aye, aye, sir!' said Mr Salt, and he and Miss Pepper heaved on the rolling-pin, once more lifting the Gingerbread Man to the High Shelf. They waited anxiously below.

The Gingerbread Man tiptoed up to the Old Bag's door. He was determined to make her help, but couldn't help feeling nervous.

He knocked once. Then again. And a third time.

Suddenly the door opened. 'Clear off!' screeched the Old Bag.

'No, please!' said the Gingerbread Man.

'Clear off!' repeated the Old Bag. 'And if you ever come on my shelf again, I'll . . .'

'I need your help!' cried the Gingerbread Man.

The Old Bag hesitated. 'What?'

'I need your help.'

'What for?'

'It's Cuckoo,' said the Gingerbread Man.

The Old Bag exploded. 'That noisy bird again? I helped him when you helped yourself to my honey.'

'He's been poisoned!' cried the Gingerbread Man.

'How dare you!' yelled the Old Bag. 'My honey is pure and healthgiving.'

'Not by your honey, by the Big Ones,' said the Gingerbread Man. 'They put poison on the honey. Look!' And he led her gently to the edge of the shelf.

The Old Bag looked down and saw the poison still scattered over the work top and the honey. 'But why?' she asked, calmer now.

'They wanted to get rid of Sleek the Mouse.'

The Old Bag eyed him nervously. 'Mouse, what mouse?' she whispered.

'Sleek,' said the Gingerbread Man. 'The mouse that's trying to eat me.'

'Eat you? Where?' The Old Bag looked around, wild-eyed. 'Has he followed you?'

'No,' said the Gingerbread Man. 'He probably went home when he saw the poison pouring down.'

'I hate mice,' said the Old Bag, trembling at the thought. 'Vicious creatures. They try to chew my perforations.'

A noise made them both jump. They turned to see something pushing its way between the herb jars.

'OK Ginger, don't move!' threatened Sleek. 'Show for a timedown . . . I mean, time for a showdown!'

48

'Aaaaaaaaaaah!' screamed the Old Bag. 'A mouse! Help! Help!' Terrified, she gathered in her perforations as Sleek advanced towards them.

The Gingerbread Man tried to sound brave. 'Go away, Sleek. I'm not frightened of you.'

'No?' grinned Sleek. 'Reckoned you were safe up here, huh? Reckoned I couldn't climb dressers too? Think again, Ginger. I used the back entrance.'

In between the herb jars the Gingerbread Man could see another mouse hole nibbled through the back of the dresser.

'Get rid of him!' wailed the Old Bag, making herself as small as possible behind the Gingerbread Man.

'You've had your fun, Ginger,' drawled Sleek. 'Now it's my turn. I'm starving!'

The Gingerbread Man stood his ground.

'You may be hungry, but try as you can,
You'll never eat the Gingerbread Man!'

Chapter 4

The Gingerbread Man walked slowly towards Sleek, who walked slowly towards him. The Old Bag scuttled back to her teapot to watch the battle in safety.

Sleek pounced. The Gingerbread Man dodged out of the way. Sleek pounced again. And again the Gingerbread Man avoided him. The third time they joined in combat. Sleek's paws grabbed the Gingerbread Man's hands in a trial of strength. First the Gingerbread Man appeared to be stronger. Sleek strained and squeaked. Then the Gingerbread Man seemed to tire. Back and forth they pulled and pushed as back and forth their luck swung. But with a final effort, Sleek forced the Gingerbread Man backwards over the edge of the shelf.

The Gingerbread Man hung on desperately as Sleek tried to heave him off. Down below Mr Salt and Miss Pepper heard the struggle and watched in horror.

The Old Bag, peeping out from under the teapot lid, saw that the Gingerbread Man was losing the fight. She knew she must help him. Terrified, she crept out of the teapot, grabbed Sleek's tail and pulled it. Hard.

'Ow!' howled Sleek, and loosened his grip on the Gingerbread Man, who wasted no time in escaping. Furious, Sleek watched him disappear through the mouse hole behind the herb jars. He turned to the Old Bag.

'You miserable Old Bag,' he squealed. 'You'll pay for that!'

He sprang towards her. She backed away, screaming. He sprang again, forcing her towards the edge.

On the work top below, Mr Salt and Miss Pepper watched, powerless to help. Suddenly, the Gingerbread Man darted through the mouse hole by the plate, having used Sleek's back route. He looked up. The Old Bag was clinging on to the edge of the shelf for dear life. The Gingerbread Man had an idea. He grabbed the tea cloth off Herr Von Cuckoo, who was still lying unconscious on the work top, and carried it to Mr Salt and Miss Pepper. Together they all

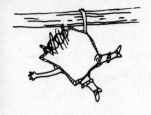

stretched it out under the shelf, just as the Old Bag lost her grip and fell, with a blood-curdling scream. She dropped safely into the tea cloth and allowed herself to be lowered to the work top. Mr Salt and Miss Pepper helped her up.

Sleek looked down from the High Shelf.

'I've been boozlebammed! I mean bamboozled!' he squealed. 'You dirty, stinking rats! There were two of you against one of me! It wasn't fair!'

The Gingerbread Man ran up to the High Shelf again, using Sleek's back entrance.

'All right, Sleek,' he shouted. 'One against one. That's fair.'

The fight broke out again. Sleek pounced. The Gingerbread Man dodged aside. Then he ran towards the Old Bag's teapot. Sleek followed. The Old Bag had left her front door ajar. The Gingerbread Man managed to open it just as Sleek pounced again. Jumping aside, the Ginger-bread Man saw Sleek hurtle past him – straight into the teapot. He quickly slammed the door shut, and wedged a box of matches under the handle to stop Sleek escaping.

Down below, the others clapped and cheered. The Gingerbread Man bowed.

'Thank you! Thank you!' he called down. 'All right, Old Bag?'

'No!' wailed the Old Bag. 'You've shut him in my teapot. There's a mouse in my house!'

'Oh, sorry,' said the Gingerbread Man. 'I'll let him out, shall I?'

'What?'

'Let him come down and nibble your perforations.'

'No, no,' said the Old Bag hastily. 'Leave him.'

'Some folk are never satisfied,' said the Gingerbread Man.

'I am, I am,' said the Old Bag. 'Thank you. Thank you *all* for saving me.'

The Old Bag had never been known to say 'thank you' before.

Mr Salt felt a little uncomfortable. 'Our duty, ma'am,' he said eventually. 'Anyone in danger on the High Shelf . . .'

'But you'd rather it hadn't been me, eh?' asked the Old Bag.

'No, but . . .' Mr Salt hesitated.

'You don't like me, do you?' asked the Old Bag.

Mr Salt didn't know what to say. The Old Bag went on: 'You think I'm a miserable Old Bag who doesn't deserve saving! Eh?'

There was an embarrassed pause. Then, the Old Bag spoke.

'Well, you're right. All this time I've kept myself to myself and then complained that I was lonely. Stupid. I can see that now.'

Mr Salt smiled. 'Well, ma'am,' he said, 'crisis brings folk together, so they say!' He offered her a hand of friendship. She shook it gratefully.

'Thank you,' she whispered.

Miss Pepper was wrapping the tea cloth around Herr Von Cuckoo again. He groaned.

'He's getting worse,' called Miss Pepper to the others. Mr Salt ran to help, but knew there was nothing he could do.

The Old Bag looked over at Herr Von Cuckoo. She thought for a moment, then called to the Gingerbread Man, who was still on guard outside the teapot on the shelf above. 'You said that bird was poisoned?'

'Yes, by the Big Ones,' said the Gingerbread Man. 'And they'll throw him in the Dustbin if he's not better when they come down. But, as you said, his cuckoos are very noisy. Good riddance.'

The Old Bag looked at her new-found friends. She couldn't just stand by and watch that bird get worse.

'May I examine Herr Von Cuckoo?' she asked. 'I may be able to help.'

Mr Salt and Miss Pepper moved aside as the Old Bag gave Herr Von Cuckoo a swift examination. After listening to his chest, looking in his mouth and checking his reflexes, she announced that she might be able to cure him, using a special medicine made up of a mixture of her herbs. She shouted instructions to the others and they all eagerly helped.

55

The Gingerbread Man collected the ingredients from the herb jars and threw them down to Miss Pepper, who carefully put them in an egg cup that Mr Salt found near the transistor radio.

The Old Bag explained all the good things her herbs could do, reciting an ancient recipe.

'Dill
Helps you sleep when you're ill
Horseradish
Eradicates the pain
Sage
Helps you live to old age

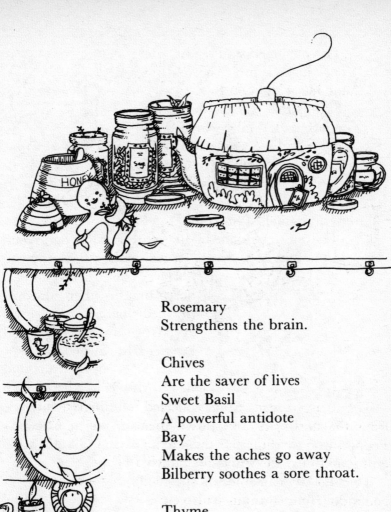

Rosemary
Strengthens the brain.

Chives
Are the saver of lives
Sweet Basil
A powerful antidote
Bay
Makes the aches go away
Bilberry soothes a sore throat.

Thyme
Puts you back in your prime
Witch Hazel
The antiseptic brew
Mint
Gives the eyes a fresh glint
Cinnamon
Fends off the 'flu.'

The medicine was ready. 'Herr Von Cuckoo must now drink,' announced the Old Bag.

From the shelf above, the Gingerbread Man watched Mr Salt and Miss Pepper help Herr Von Cuckoo to the egg cup.

'Drink this, Cuckoo,' said Miss Pepper.

'Ugh!' said Cuckoo, turning up his beak. The medicine smelled horrid.

'The nastier it smells, the more good it does you!' said the Old Bag. 'Drink. It will make you sleepy.'

Herr Von Cuckoo took a deep breath, then downed the medicine. Soon he felt his eyelids getting heavier and heavier. He yawned.

'That's good,' said the Old Bag. 'Mr Salt, please help me lead him home.'

'Aye, aye, ma'am,' said Mr Salt, taking Cuckoo's arm.

'Will he get better?' asked Miss Pepper.

'I think so,' said the Old Bag. 'But not for a few hours. I'll stay with him.'

Mr Salt helped her help Cuckoo into his clock. Then she climbed in too.

'Thank you, Old Bag,' said Mr Salt warmly.

The Old Bag looked at him. 'Thank me when he's better,' she snapped, and shut the door.

'Well, well,' sighed Mr Salt, returning to Miss Pepper by the rolling-pin. 'What a night!'

Miss Pepper smiled. She had often complained how boring life was on the dresser. But tonight she had had more excitement than she could have dreamed of. 'It's been a wonderful night,' she cried. 'I do hope it hasn't finished yet!'

'It's hardly started!' called a voice from the High Shelf. Mr Salt and Miss Pepper jumped and looked up.

'It's only the Gingerbread Man,' said Mr Salt.

'I'd forgotten you were up there,' said Miss Pepper.

'You've forgotten something else as well,' called down the Gingerbread Man. 'Sleek the Mouse is up here too! In the Old Bag's teapot. What are we going to do with him?'

'Give him the poison,' suggested Miss Pepper.

'He wouldn't fall for that,' said the Gingerbread Man. 'He saw it being put down.'

'You'll just have to let him out, then order him home,' said Mr Salt.

'I can't do that!' cried the Gingerbread Man. 'He's starving. He won't stop to listen. He'll just start nibbling. Me!'

'Where does he live, anyway?' asked Mr Salt.

'Behind the dresser,' replied the Gingerbread Man. Suddenly an idea came to him. 'Wait a minute,' he said. 'He's only here because I was curious and let him in. But if we could get him back through his hole up here and block it up, *and* push the plate back down below, he'd be shut out.'

Mr Salt thought about this. He saw a problem. 'Sleek would never fall for that,' he said. 'You just said he's starving. He won't disembark from the dresser till he's had his nibble.'

'Well,' shouted the Gingerbread Man, 'he's not nibbling *me*!'

'We won't let him,' said Miss Pepper. She had an idea. 'First, we'll let him out of the teapot, next we'll have to catch him and *then* we'll have to force him back through the hole.'

'But how can we catch him?' asked Mr Salt.

Everybody thought hard. The Gingerbread Man, who was sitting on the edge of the High Shelf, suddenly noticed the large mug hanging from the cup-hook next to him.

'Hey!' he cried. 'How about a mug mouse-trap?'

'How do you mean?' asked Mr Salt.

'Turn the mug upside down and drop it over Sleek,' said the Gingerbread Man. 'Catch him under it.'

Mr Salt and Miss Pepper thought it was worth trying. They worked out a way of lowering the mug to the work top. The Gingerbread Man tied his loop of string round the handle of the mug and gently slid the mug off the hook. Then, making sure the string ran over the cup-hook, Mr Salt and Miss Pepper gradually let out the string from below. The mug was safely lowered to the work top and turned upside down. The loop of string was still tied to the handle, and then went over the cup-hook and back down to Mr Salt.

'Heave on the halyard!' ordered Mr Salt, and he

and Miss Pepper pulled on the string. The string pulled on the handle and tipped the mug on to one side, leaving a gap – just enough for a mouse to crawl under.

'Excellent!' said Mr Salt. 'Right, Gingerbread Man, let him out of the teapot. We're ready for him.'

'Hang on!' said the Gingerbread Man.

'Exactly,' said Mr Salt, looking at the string. 'Hang on the halyard.'

'No,' said the Gingerbread Man. 'Hang on. Problem.'

'Problem?'

'How do we make sure Sleek gets in the right position for the trap to work?'

'He's right,' said Miss Pepper. 'We can't just expect Sleek to run under the mug.'

'Mmm,' thought Mr Salt. 'What would make Sleek want to go under the mug?'

'Food!' cried the Gingerbread Man. 'He's hungry. He's bound to sniff around for food and . . .' his mind was now racing . . . 'suppose he had to go under the mug to get it . . .'

'Yes,' said Mr Salt. 'Now, what might he fancy?'

'The Big Ones sometimes catch mice using cheese,' said Miss Pepper.

'No cheese aboard,' said Mr Salt.

'*I* know!' cried Miss Pepper, and ran to the back of the dresser. She hurried back clutching a juicy-looking sweet. A fruit pastille with a sugar coating. It looked very tempting. 'There's half a tube left,' said Miss Pepper. 'The Big Ones will never notice one's missing.' She carefully pushed it under the mug.

Mr Salt was still hauling on the halyard. 'Hurry up!' he shouted. 'This is heavy.'

Miss Pepper ran to help him. The Gingerbread Man tip-toed to the teapot, pulled aside the matchbox jamming the door, and hid.

Sleek, inside the teapot, had tried everything to get out, but no amount of pushing or shoving or nibbling had helped him escape. Now he heard noises outside the door. What was going on? He gingerly touched the door. It moved! A stronger push and it opened. He scampered outside on to the shelf, happy to be free, but suspicious of trickery. He sniffed nervously. Nothing stirred on the dresser. Sleek pricked up his ears. Not a sound.

'Where's that Mingerbread Gan? ... I mean Gingerbread Man?' he said to himself. 'I've had enough of his tricks and I'm starving.' Sniff, sniff, sniff. He stopped. 'What's that swell smell?' Sniff, sniff. 'Kind of juicy and crunchy and ...' He followed the smell until he came to the edge of the shelf. 'It's down there,' he thought, 'and it smells delicious!'

He sped eagerly to the side of the dresser, and, digging his claws into the wood, swung his way down to the work top. With a few inches to go he was so excited he lost his grip and fell. But he rolled over a couple of times and wasn't hurt at all.

'Where is it? Where is it?' he muttered to himself, sniffing the mouth-watering smell of the sweet.

The fruity smell got stronger and stronger. Sleek arrived near the mug. He poked his twitching nose and trembling whiskers underneath.

'Here it is!' he said to himself, eyes bright with

anticipation. 'It's a fruit pastille! Blackcurrant flavour! My favourite!'

He started to go under the mug. He stopped. 'Could this be a trick?' he thought. 'A trap?' But the thought of that chewy pastille was too strong. He scuttled under the mug and started tucking in.

'Now!' yelled the Gingerbread Man, watching from the High Shelf.

Mr Salt and Miss Pepper loosened their hold on the string and down crashed the mug. Sleek was trapped. All cheered.

'Well done!' cried the Gingerbread Man. 'And thank you. I'd have been nibbled if you two hadn't helped!'

Mr Salt untied the string and threw the loop up to the Gingerbread Man. 'We'll let you down, now,' he called.

'Hang on!' cried the Gingerbread Man. 'I haven't blocked the hole up here yet.' With a mighty effort he heaved the honey pot against it. Sleek could never push past that. Then, using the rolling-pin capstan, Mr Salt and Miss Pepper lowered the Gingerbread

63

Man to the work top. They all carefully slid the mug, with Sleek underneath, over to the mouse hole by the plate. With great care they managed to tip up the mug towards the hole. Sleek saw his chance, sped out from under the mug, and away through the hole. The Gingerbread Man rolled back the plate to where he had first found it. Sleek was well and truly shut out.

They all cheered.

'Shhhhh!' A voice came from the cuckoo clock. 'Quiet!' whispered the Old Bag, shutting the door and making her way towards them. 'Herr Von Cuckoo is asleep.'

'Sleek's gone home!' cried the Gingerbread Man.

The Old Bag jumped. '*My* home?' she snapped.

'No,' replied the Gingerbread Man. 'Behind the dresser.'

'Good riddance!' said the Old Bag.

'How is Cuckoo?' enquired Mr Salt.

'Much better,' replied the Old Bag. 'But he must have hush. If he can sleep until just before eight o'clock he should be fine again.'

'Hooray!' cried the Gingerbread Man.

'Shhhhh!' went the others.

They were all tired after the adventures of the night. So they huddled together around the rolling-pin and went to sleep.

The hands on the cuckoo clock showed the minutes ticking by. Hours passed. As the early morning light crept through the kitchen window, nothing stirred. But just before eight o'clock, the cuckoo clock door opened and Herr Von Cuckoo popped out. He felt much better. There was just time to test his voice before the Big Ones came downstairs.

'Mi, mi, mi, mi. La, la, la, la, la, teeee!' The notes sounded clear and tuneful. His throat didn't feel sore any more. 'Cuckoo! Cuckoo!' Nothing wrong at all. 'The toad has flown!' cried Herr Von Cuckoo. 'My voice is found!'

The others woke up and congratulated Cuckoo. He thanked them for helping him, particularly the Gingerbread Man for fetching the honey, and the Old Bag for using her herbs to make him better.

Suddenly they heard familiar muffled clumping noises. The Big Ones were coming downstairs. Mr Salt and Miss Pepper hurried back to the spot where the Big Ones had left them yesterday. They had no time to put the envelope back between them, but hoped the Big Ones wouldn't notice. The Gingerbread Man dashed back to his place behind the rolling-pin and lay down. The Old Bag, unable to go home to the High Shelf, hid behind a plate.

They all whispered 'good luck' to Herr Von Cuckoo as he popped back inside his clock.

The kitchen door opened.

'HURRY UP, DEAR,' boomed Mrs Big One. 'WE'LL BE LATE.'

'SORRY, DARLING,' echoed Mr Big One. 'I MUST HAVE OVERSLEPT.'

'WELL, I'VE GOT TO BE AT WORK BY NINE,' said Mrs Big One.

'NO TIME FOR BREAKFAST, THEN,' said Mr Big One.

'ANY SIGN OF THAT MOUSE, DEAR?' asked Mrs Big One, nervously.

'NO, DARLING, HE WOULDN'T DARE COME BACK AFTER THE WAY WE SENT HIM PACKING,' replied Mr Big One.

'Huh!' thought the Gingerbread Man, 'the way *we* sent him packing, you mean!'

At eight o'clock on the dot, Herr Von Cuckoo popped out of his front door and took a deep breath.

'Cuckoo! Cuckoo! Cuckoo! Cuckoo!'

The other dresser folk almost joined in, they so wanted him to cuckoo well.

'Cuckoo! Cuckoo! Cuckoo! Cuckoo!'

'DID YOU HEAR THAT, DARLING?' boomed Mr Big One. 'EIGHT PERFECT WORKING ORDER CUCKOOS.'

'HE'S NOT PAST IT AFTER ALL!' echoed Mrs Big One. 'NO DUSTBIN FOR HIM!'

Herr Von Cuckoo beamed a huge smile. In his excitement he forgot to go back in his clock.

'HE PROBABLY HAD A BIT OF FLUFF IN HIS WORKS,' said Mr Big One.

'How dare you!' thought Herr Von Cuckoo. But he didn't mind. The Big Ones would never know the truth. Why should they?

The Big Ones turned to leave.

'DO YOU WANT THE GINGERBREAD MAN TO NIBBLE IN THE CAR?' asked Mrs Big One.

'THAT'S AN IDEA!' replied Mr Big One. 'IF THERE'S NO TIME FOR BREAKFAST...'

The Gingerbread Man trembled. The other dresser folk were frightened too. They didn't want him to be eaten.

'HANG ON!' said Mr Big One. 'HE'S PROBABLY ALL GERMY. THAT MOUSE MUST HAVE RUN ALL OVER HIM.'

'UGH, YOU'RE RIGHT, DEAR,' said Mrs Big One. 'DON'T EAT HIM. MIGHT MAKE YOURSELF ILL.'

The dresser folk smiled with relief.

'YES,' said Mr Big One. 'I'LL THROW HIM IN THE DUSTBIN.'

The dresser folk stopped smiling. The Gingerbread Man trembled again. But he was saved by Mrs Big One.

'OH NO, DON'T DO THAT,' she cried. 'HE'S NICE. HE'S GOT A CHEEKY FACE.' (She forgot *she* hadn't given him a face.) 'LET'S KEEP HIM. HE CAN STAND ON THE SHELF

NEXT TO THE TEAPOT. COME ON DEAR, WE'LL BE LATE.'

Off they went, slamming the kitchen door behind them. Straight away the dresser folk cheered and jumped for joy. They congratulated Cuckoo for singing so well and told the Gingerbread Man how glad they were that he could stay among them.

'I'm not to be beaten, and not to be eaten!' he kept shouting.

'A happy end to the voyage!' smiled Mr Salt.

'Happy?' shrieked a voice from behind a plate. Out crept the Old Bag, looking very cross. 'First that bird is better,' she moaned, 'and second, I have to share my shelf with a Gingerbread Man. You think I'm *happy*?' She paused, then smiled. 'I'm delighted, thrilled!'

Everyone cheered.

'And, Gingerbread Man,' the Old Bag went on. 'If you don't visit me at least twice every day, there'll be trouble!'

'Trouble?' cried the Gingerbread Man. 'I can cope with trouble. Your fortune-telling was right. You said –

"When trouble comes, if you can cope
    Three lives will shortly find new hope."'

'One is me,' said Herr Von Cuckoo. 'I escaped the Dustbin!'

'Two is me,' said the Gingerbread Man. 'I escaped being eaten.'

'And three?' asked Mr Salt.

'Three,' said the Old Bag, 'is . . . me!'

'You?' asked Miss Pepper. 'What did you escape?'

The Old Bag smiled. 'I escaped . . . from myself,' she said. 'And found you . . . my friends.'

Everyone cheered again.

The Gingerbread Man turned on the transistor radio. Music blared out. Nobody stopped him. It didn't matter now. The Big Ones had gone to work. 'Let's have a party!' he cried.

'Now?' asked Mr Salt.

'Why not?' said Miss Pepper. 'A celebration! To celebrate the most exciting day on this dresser I can remember!

The day that began
With the Gingerbread Man!'

Recipe

If you would like to make your own Gingerbread Man, do please ask a grown-up to help you with this special recipe.

Ingredients

225g (8oz) plain flour
1 level teaspoon bicarbonate of soda
2 level teaspoons ground ginger
100g (4oz) butter or margarine
85g (3oz) soft brown sugar
3 tablespoons golden syrup
1 egg
currants
glacé cherries

1. Grease baking sheets. If you haven't a gingerbread man cutter, cut a shape from greaseproof paper for a pattern.

2. Mix flour, soda and ginger, sieve into bowl. Cut in fat and rub into dry ingredients till mixture looks like breadcrumbs.

3. Mix in sugar. Warm syrup in a basin over hot water, beat in egg. Add to bowl mixing to a pliable dough.

4. Knead lightly on floured surface, roll out to 0.5cm ($\frac{1}{8}''$) thick. Cut round paper with knife (or use cutter).

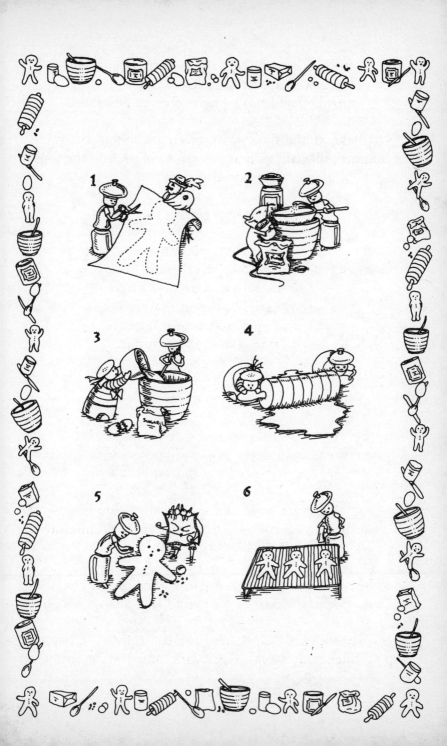

5. Lift men on to baking sheets with palette knife, keeping well apart. Mark eyes and nose with currants, and use a cherry for the mouth.

6. Bake at 190°C (475°F), gas mark 5, for 10–15 minutes till pale golden brown. Cool slightly then carefully move to wire rack.

Some other Young Puffins

UPSIDE DOWN STORIES
Donald Bisset

Brilliant nonsense tales to delight children, telling about such oddities as an inexperienced apple tree which grows squirrels instead of apples!

DORRIE AND THE BIRTHDAY EGGS
Patricia Coombs

When the eggs for the Big Witch's birthday cake get broken by mistake, Dorrie sets off to buy some more from the Egg Witch. But her errand takes her through the forest, and lurking there is Thinnever Vetch, all ready to make mischief . . .

ALLOTMENT LANE SCHOOL AGAIN
Margaret Joy

It's always fun in Miss Mee's class and now the holidays are over and everyone is glad to be back at Allotment Lane School again. Fourteen lively stories about Class 1 and their friends.

HANK PRANK AND HOT HENRIETTA
Jules Older

Hank and his hot tempered sister, Henrietta, are always getting themselves into trouble but the doings of this terrible pair make for an entertaining series of adventures.

CHRIS AND THE DRAGON
Fay Sampson

Chris always seems to be in trouble but he does try extra hard to be good when he is chosen to play Joseph in the school nativity play. This hilarious story ends with a glorious celebration of the Chinese New Year.

ONE NIL

Tony Bradman

Dave Brown is mad about football and when he learns that the England squad are to train at the local City ground he thinks up a brilliant plan to overcome his parents' objections and get him to the ground to see them.

ON THE NIGHT WATCH

Hannah Cole

A group of children and their parents occupy their tiny school in an effort to prevent its closure.

FIONA FINDS HER TONGUE

Diana Hendry

At home Fiona is a chatterbox but whenever she goes out she just won't say a word. How she overcomes her shyness and 'finds her tongue' is told in this charming book.

IT'S TOO FRIGHTENING FOR ME!

Shirley Hughes

The eerie old house gives Jim and Arthur the creeps. But somehow they just can't resist poking around it, even when a mysterious white face appears at the window! A deliciously scary story – for brave readers only!

THE CONKER AS HARD AS A DIAMOND

Chris Powling

Last conker season little Alpesh had lost every single game! But this year it's going to be different and he's going to be Conker Champion of the Universe! The trouble is, only a conker as hard as a diamond will make it possible – and where on earth is he going to find one?

THE GHOST AT NO. 13

Gyles Brandreth

Hamlet Brown's sister, Susan, is just too perfect. Everything she does is praised and Halmet is in despair – until a ghost comes to stay for a holiday and helps him to find an exciting idea for his school project!

RADIO DETECTIVE

John Escott

A piece of amazing deduction by the Roundbay Radio Detective when Donald, the radio's young presenter, solves a mystery but finds out more than anyone expects.

RAGDOLLY ANNA'S CIRCUS

Jean Kenward

Made only from a morsel of this and a tatter of that, Ragdolly Anna is a very special doll and the six stories in this book are all about her adventures.

SEE YOU AT THE MATCH

Margaret Joy

Six delightful stories about football. Whether spectator, player, winner or loser these short, easy stories for young readers are a must for all football fans.

THE RAILWAY CAT'S SECRET

Phyllis Arkle

Stories about Alfie, the Railway Cat, and his sworn enemy Hack the porter. Alfie tries to win over Hack by various means with often hilarious results.

WORD PARTY

Richard Edwards

A delightful collection of poems – lively, snappy and easy to read.

THE THREE AND MANY WISHES OF JASON REID

Hazel Hutchins

Jason is eleven and a very good thinker so when he is granted three wishes he is very wary indeed. After all, he knows the tangles that happen in fairy stories!

THE AIR-RAID SHELTER

Jeremy Strong

Adam and his sister Rachel find a perfect place for their secret camp in the grounds of a deserted house, until they are discovered by their sworn enemies and things go from bad to worse.